Video Game Designer

Other titles in the *Cutting Edge Careers* series include:

Big Data Analyst

Cybersecurity Analyst

Robotics Engineer

Software Engineer

Virtual Reality Developer

CUTTING EDGE
Careers

Video Game Designer

Stephanie Watson

ReferencePoint
Press®

San Diego, CA

Dedication

To my brilliant, talented son Jake—my video game guru.

© 2018 ReferencePoint Press, Inc.
Printed in the United States

For more information, contact:
ReferencePoint Press, Inc.
PO Box 27779
San Diego, CA 92198
www.ReferencePointPress.com

LIBRARY OF CONGRESS CATALOGING-IN-PUBLICATION DATA

Name: Watson, Stephanie, 1969– author.
Title: Video game designer/by Stephanie Watson.
Description: San Diego, CA: ReferencePoint Press, 2018. | Series: Cutting Edge Careers | Audience: Grades 9 to 12.
Identifiers: LCCN 2016052546 (print) | LCCN 2016055937 (ebook) | ISBN 9781682821848 (hardback) | ISBN 9781682821855 (eBook)
Subjects: LCSH: Video games—Design—Vocational guidance—Juvenile literature. | Video games industry--Vocational guidance--Juvenile literature. | Computer games—Programming—Vocational guidance—Juvenile literature.
Classification: LCC GV1469.3 .W465 2018 (print) | LCC GV1469.3 (ebook) | DDC 794.8/1536--dc23
LC record available at https://lccn.loc.gov/2016052546

CONTENTS

VIDEO GAME DESIGNER AT A GLANCE

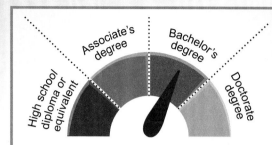

Minimum Educational Requirements

(Gauge showing: High school diploma or equivalent, Associate's degree, Bachelor's degree, Doctorate degree — needle pointing to Bachelor's degree)

Personal Qualities

- ☑ Creativity
- ☑ Teamwork
- ☑ Detail oriented
- ☑ Problem-solving skills
- ☑ Organized
- ☑ Technical skills
- ☑ Programming skills

Working Conditions

Office

Salary

About $73,000

233,000
Number of jobs

New jobs by 2018
8,000
Future Job Outlook

Source: Bureau of Labor Statistics, *Occupational Outlook Handbook.* www.bls.gov

Life as a Video Game Designer

You are the number one quarterback in the NFL, about to face the toughest defensive line in the league as thousands of fans scream for you in the stands. . . . You have just emerged from a fallout shelter in the year 2287, more than two hundred years after Earth has been decimated by a nuclear war, and now you must set out to avenge the deaths of your spouse and son. . . . You are a Pokémon hunter, finding and catching these colorful creatures wherever they might hide. . . . You are an unlikely hero named Mario, fighting off the evil turtle king Bowser's henchmen in Mushroom Kingdom to rescue Princess Peach.

These are not the story lines of a movie or book. They are the plots of popular video games. Video games have stories, scenes, and characters just like movies do, but they add the element of control, as players direct every moment of the action.

The Video Game Industry Today

Since the 1970s, when the first video game—*Pong*—was released, the industry has come a long way. From little more than a couple of moving white lines and a dot against a black screen, video gaming has evolved into three-dimensional and highly realistic virtual worlds. The new generation of virtual reality games even lets players step inside the action.

Video games today are more than just entertainment—they are big business. More than half of Americans regularly play video games. In part, the popularity has been driven by the fact that people can now play these games almost anywhere. You can shoot aliens or zombies on your home television. You can build a virtual world with a team of people from around the world over the Internet. You can immerse yourself in a three-dimensional car race via a virtual reality headset. You can slingshot many different colored birds at pigs on your smartphone.

Indeed, the versatility of the medium has introduced a whole new audience to gaming. "20 years ago, when you think of gamers it was a bunch of geeks in their rooms playing PC games—it was a very narrow group of people," says Sean Lee, chief corporate development officer at Wargaming. "What you're seeing is that explosion of demographic outside that core group. It's one of the fastest growing industries in the world because of that massive explosion of the audience base."[1]

People of all ages, from all walks of life, and from just about every country on the planet play video games. Their dedication to this form of entertainment has transformed video gaming from a hobby into a multibillion-dollar industry.

The Video Game Designer

Creating the magical new worlds and fantastic story lines featured in video games requires a team of creative and technical professionals—writers, animators, programmers, and sound designers. The person responsible for overseeing every aspect of the video game—from the script to the final product—is the video game designer. Designers are central to this industry. Their creativity, vision, and technical skills bring video games to life. They invent the incredibly complex and high-level worlds and story lines that transform everyday people into superheroes, sports superstars, and super villains.

Ultimately, designers create an experience that players will not soon forget. "What you're responsible for as a game designer is whether a game is fun or not," says Paolo Malabuyo, lead design program manager for Xbox and Microsoft. "When you listen to a group of people who just played a fun multiplayer

> "What you're responsible for as a game designer is whether a game is fun or not. When you listen to a group of people who just played a fun multiplayer game together, it sounds as if they are telling the story of something they just did in reality."[2]
>
> —Paolo Malabuyo, lead design program manager for Xbox and Microsoft

Making Your Own Game

If you are passionate about gaming, it is never too early to start creating your own video games. Come up with a story line you have never seen before or create a sequel to one of your favorite existing games. Even if you know nothing about programming, online tools like GameMaker, Unity, and Cocos can help you get your first game off the ground.

You can design games on your own or form a development team. "Find other people who want to make games and make a game together," suggests game developer and software engineer Allison Salmon. "Very few games are made by one person alone. Good places to meet other developers are at local meet-ups, game jams, on Twitter and in other online communities."

Quoted in Keith Stuart, "How to Get into the Games Industry—an Insiders' Guide," *Guardian*, March 20, 2014. www.theguardian.com.

game together, it sounds as if they are telling the story of something they just did in reality."[2]

If you have grown up playing video games and you love the medium, video game designer might be the job for you. However, having a career in video games requires more than just loving gaming and logging thousands of hours on a computer or Xbox. "I think the biggest misconception is that the industry will just 'happen' to you if you play a lot of games," says Tomm Hulett, a veteran in the industry. "You don't get to make games by sitting around playing RPGs [role-playing games] and dreaming. . . . You have to get out there and work hard."[3]

That hard work starts with getting a degree in video game design and having a background in programming, art, or writing. From there, the typical way into the industry is to get a job with an established video game company or studio and to work your way up from an entry-level game tester position to senior or lead designer. The ultimate goal for many designers is to start their own studio, so they can have complete control over the games they make.

However, you do not have to wait until you have been in the industry for years to make a game. You can start designing your own video games today and distribute them online with the help of a few tools that are available on the Internet.

CHAPTER 1

What Does a Video Game Designer Do?

Whenever you play a video game—whether it is *Pokémon*, *Minecraft*, *Candy Crush Saga*, or *Madden NFL 17*—every creature you catch, building you create, or pass you throw is the direct result of a video game designer's work. Designers do everything from coming up with the original game concept to deciding how a character will look, sound, and move.

The Role of the Video Game Designer

Executives and managers at a video game development company will usually kick off the entire process by defining the game's concept. They do so after conducting lots of research to find out what types of games players want to buy. Or they may base the game on a successful movie or franchise that already exists—like *Star Wars*, *Madden NFL*, or *Mario Kart*.

Once the concept is set, the lead video game designer takes over. He or she develops the concept, fleshing it out further. What is the goal of the game? Is it a football game, a first-person shooter game, a simulation game, or a role-playing action game? Will the player solve puzzles or go on a quest to defeat a horde of flesh-eating zombies? Is it designed for a single player or multiple players?

The Stages of Video Game Design

In the earliest stages of game development, a team of designers focuses the game to the desired audience. For example, a Disney game filled with cartoon characters will have a very different audience (young children) than a war game with lots of simulated violence and blood (adults). Every part of the game must be appropriate for the desired audience.

Designers also need to consider how much money it will cost to make the game. This is called the budget. Some larger companies have millions to spend on production. Smaller independent game studios may have only a few thousand dollars. Designers must create the best possible game with the amount of money they have.

They also have to figure out what kind of platform the game will run on. Will they design it for a console like Xbox, PlayStation, or Nintendo DS? Or will it run on a computer, smartphone, or virtual reality headset? Will it be a multiplatform game, meaning that it can run on more than one of these devices?

Designers have to understand what kinds of programming languages and technologies they need to take the game from concept to millions of screens around the world. And they need to set a deadline for doing so—a date by which the game needs to be finished so it can get shipped to stores or published online.

> "In the early stages of design . . . everyone is just trying to think of the coolest system possible to accomplish the game's goals."[4]
>
> —Kurt Tillmanns, game designer for Iron Galaxy Studios

Each step of the production process is detailed in a document known as the game design bible. It contains a rundown of everything that goes into the game, including the concept, plot, characters, levels, and rules. Sometimes many different designers, artists, writers, programmers, and other staff members end up working on different pieces of the same game. The game design bible ensures they are all on the same page and working toward the same goals.

Game Plot and Characters

Once the fundamentals of theme, platform, budget, and timeline are decided on, the concept work—or brainstorming—begins. This is the creative part of the process. "In the early stages of design . . . everyone is just trying to think of the coolest system

Part of designing a video game is deciding in what sort of environment the action should take place. Some designers create whole new worlds while others choose more earthly settings.

possible to accomplish the game's goals,"[4] says Kurt Tillmanns, a designer at Iron Galaxy Studios, a company that has produced games like *Divekick* and *Wreckateer*.

An individual designer or team of designers creates the plot, characters, and rules of each game. Will the world be populated by animated creatures or realistic-looking humans? Will players have to save the world from alien invaders? Will they have to lead their favorite NBA team into the playoffs? Or will they have to navigate a magical kingdom filled with wizards and witches?

Designers must think of and create every element of a game. They decide what each screen and level looks like and what puzzles and challenges players will face on each level. They determine how hard it will be to defeat every enemy, how the story will move forward, and what goals players will need to accomplish to win the game. Designers work with writers and artists to create what is called a storyboard—preliminary sketches that depict

Video Game Designers Do More than Play Games

One of the biggest misconceptions about video game designers is the idea that they sit around all day playing video games. Though game play is part of the development process, it is not the same as sitting at home and playing video games for fun. The work can be very tedious. Often a designer is focused on the same small section of a game for hours, even days, at a time.

There is a lot of pressure on designers to get the game right. Thousands or even millions of dollars are at stake with each game. "With games, you make or break your sale with every single person who comes to the store, picks up your box and tries to decide if it's a game worth playing," says Paolo Malabuyo. "We spend three years working on it, to come up with cool innovative ideas that will compel people to fork over the money and go on a ride. It's harder than it sounds!"

Quoted in AllArtSchools, "Video Game Designer Profile: Paolo Malabuyo." www.allartschools.com.

each scene in the game and make up a sort of road map.

They also have to develop characters to inhabit the world they have created. Designing a character from scratch is kind of like giving birth to a brand-new creature. The designer works with an artist to sketch out each character on paper or a computer. Characters are then fleshed out in three dimensions and are animated. The designer needs to make the characters come alive by figuring out how they talk, what moves they make (whether they punch, hit, jump, or crawl), and how each move from an opponent will affect them. "We have a set of rules that we can explore within each character," explains Brian Davis, who worked on *Luigi's Mansion* for Nintendo. "[Toad is] supposed to look like he's having fun when he's with Luigi. There are situations in the game where, if he's not connected with Luigi, we try to make him look scared or frightened, so that the player feels an emotional connection with him when you leave him."[5]

Creating characters is part of the job of game designers. They typically work with artists to flesh out the characters' personalities, movements, and interactions.

The characters also need a place to live and play—the game's environment. Designers and artists decide what this world they have invented will look like. Will it be made up of tall buildings, castles, or forests? Will it look like Earth or another planet? Every element of the environment, from the clouds in the sky to the furniture inside buildings, must be planned and defined based on the game's plot, story line, and parameters.

Implementing a Concept

Once the ideas are in place, the game is ready to start being built. This part of the process is less about creativity and more about problem solving. Conceiving of the game was all about imagining it; implementing that concept involves figuring out what problems need to be solved to make the game a reality. "Game development from a production and engineering perspective is much more structured and logic based," Tillmanns says. "As a designer let's say I come up with a system to be implemented—almost all my interaction from a development standpoint is poking holes in it and solving problems that are hard to know about earlier, during the creative process."[6] In other words, will the world and creatures actually work during play?

"Showing the game to everyone who will listen and quickly iterating [making changes] based on their feedback is how we know when we want to take an idea to the next level."[7]

—Jake Fleming, designer on *Hot Shot Santa*

Building a video game requires a team effort. Designers work with a group of artists, animators, writers, and programmers to take their concept from the page to the screen. They also rely on outside advice, or feedback, from friends, family members, and other people in the video game industry. Getting feedback is especially important in the early stages of development, when designers are testing out a new game concept. "Showing the game to everyone who will listen and quickly iterating [making changes] based on their feedback is how we know when we want to take an idea to the next level,"[7] says Jake Fleming, a designer who has worked on games like *Grilly the Cheese* and *Hot Shot Santa*.

Testing and Retesting

Next, a game enters the testing phase. In this phase, designers need to make sure the story makes sense, that players move smoothly from one level to the next, and that characters' moves and personalities fit them. They also need to ensure there are no bugs—malfunctions that could interrupt game play. Bugs can range from minor problems—like a moon appearing in the daytime sky—to major technical issues that halt play entirely.

The highly detailed and often grueling job of testing the game usually falls to quality assurance (QA) testers. QA testers play the game—or a section of it—over and over again. Their goal is to make sure everything works like the designer intended it to. Consider a basketball player in an NBA game who shoots the ball. If the ball disappears in midair, that is a bug. The game designer might also test the game, but at the very least he or she will oversee the QA testers and make sure any problems that are identified get fixed. The entire video game development process, from concept to completion, can take one to two years or even longer. Video game designers typically stay on a project until it is ready to be released.

How Do You Become a Video Game Designer?

Like many other professions, a career in video game design starts by getting a bachelor's degree. In the past, one could land a job in the gaming industry with a liberal arts degree. That is harder to do today. "I got lucky because I learned how to do the job on the job," says Kelly Murphy, a video game designer who has worked for Disney. "Nowadays there's so much competition it's not that feasible. You have so many kids going to school for this."[8]

Today many colleges and universities offer specialized video game design programs. These programs combine courses in math, programming, logic, writing, game design, two- and three-dimensional art, animation, and game testing. Getting a degree in video game design tells future employers you have all the fundamental skills to create games from start to finish. At the end of many game design programs, students typically do a final project in which they create and design their own game. Many use this as a demo to show to prospective employers when they interview.

Another option is to specialize in one area while in college, such as computer science, computer engineering, programming, writing, art, or sound design. "Get good at something related to games," Murphy says. "So if art is your thing, learn really good fine art fundamental skills. I would go to a school that has a good art program and potentially a good animation program."[9]

Then, add to your skill set. So if you major in art or computer science, learning additional skills such as writing, music, sound design, and animation can be an asset. Creative writing and scripting courses teach future designers how to develop characters and move the story forward using dialogue. Sound design classes teach students to choose the right music and sound effects to accentuate their games. Marketing classes show them how to spot trends in the industry so they can develop games that are likely to be big sellers. Though one does not need a master's degree to design games, an advanced degree can prepare future designers for a management position in which they can earn a higher salary.

Computer programming is an especially helpful skill to learn. Knowing one or more programming languages can help a game designer understand whether the elements he or she has thought up for a game can actually be implemented. Some of the languages used to create video games are Java, C++, HTML5, CSS3, and SQL. If you do not want to learn the high-level programming languages, simpler versions are available. "I've had to learn scripting, which is kind of like a layman's programming," Murphy says. "Nowadays there are a lot of scripting languages

Inside a University Video Game Design Program

What would you actually study if you attended a college video game design program? Here is a sample of the undergraduate courses offered by the University of Southern California, one of the top-ranked game design programs in the country:

- Introduction to Game Development: Learn both the technical and creative aspects of game development.
- Game Design Workshop: Discover the software and other technologies used to create video games.
- Interface Design for Games: Learn how to work in both two-dimensional and three-dimensional spaces.
- Usability Testing for Games: Find out how to test games to make sure they work and learn about the issues that affect different game interfaces.
- Business and Management of Games: Find out how to pitch a new game idea to gaming companies and get your independent projects funded.

[including C#, Python, Lua, and Javascript] that people who want to get into games but aren't really programmers can use."[10]

Play Games

If you ask video game designers about their favorite hobby, just about all of them will say they are passionate about gaming. "Developers should play games," says David Braben, founder of Frontier Games, which made *Zoo Tycoon*, *Kinectimals*, and *Planet Coaster*. "The reason they become developers should be because they are gamers. Would you expect someone making films to not have any love or appreciation of films?"[11]

When your aim is to be a video game designer, nothing can replace the experience of playing. Although game play is not the only thing necessary to be a game designer, it is as essential as getting a degree. "No college degree in itself can make you a game designer," says Allen Varney, a writer and game designer. "Good design requires creativity and independence of thought. . . . You would do better to play a lot of games, try to understand what parts of them work and don't work, and educate yourself in the subjects you'd like to cover in your games."[12]

> "Good design requires creativity and independence of thought."[12]
>
> —Allen Varney, writer and game designer

Designers also try to play as many different types of games as they can. Doing so teaches them how games are structured, what platforms are available on which to play games, and how to use technology to execute their ideas. It also offers insight into industry trends—which games are popular right now or which ones might become popular in the near future.

Become an Intern

Video game designers learn the skills they need in college, but they hone those skills out in the real world. To get such experience, many intern for a video game company while they are still in college or even in high school. Interning is one of the best ways to gain more experience and make the connections that will help you land your first job.

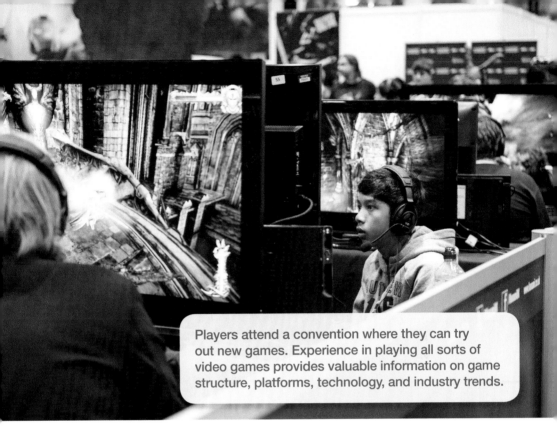

Players attend a convention where they can try out new games. Experience in playing all sorts of video games provides valuable information on game structure, platforms, technology, and industry trends.

Students who want to intern in the game industry can check with their high school or college counselor or department head. They may have connections at video game companies in the area. Students can also visit the websites of gaming companies to see if they run internship programs. Potential interns have to interview, just as they would for a full-time job. They also might need references from a professor, school counselor, or past employer.

Regardless of whether an internship is paid or unpaid, the job has many rewards. Student interns learn valuable skills to showcase on their résumés. They will likely get a credit on any game they work on. And, if they show a lot of initiative, they could end up with a full-time position at the company once they graduate. Jon Shafer interned at Firaxis Games in Maryland. He started out programming and then graduated to making scenarios and maps for the game *Civilization*. When his company started making add-on game scenarios for *Civilization IV*, they needed more designers. "That's when I got the job," he says. "I was hired on as a full-time designer after getting my degree."[13]

Make Your Own Games

If you want to make games, you do not need to wait for a company to hire you. You also do not need millions of dollars. With some hard work and time, you can make your own game using inexpensive or free game development software programs like Sploder, GameMaker, and Unity. Once you have created a game, you can publish it on your own website or submit it to an existing game company or online platform like Steam.

> "Design games on your own, even if they're card games or board games, it's almost all the same process."[14]
>
> —Abby Friesen, creator of *Reach for the Sun*

Even making low-tech games can help someone interested in video game design develop the skills needed to become a professional designer. "Design games on your own, even if they're card games or board games, it's almost all the same process," says Abby Friesen, a designer who created the award-winning *Reach for the Sun* game. "Generate ideas and practice writing them all out as though you were going to hand your written game pitch to a programmer and they were going to make it based off what you wrote."[14]

Become a Video Game Tester

One easy way for new video game designers to get their first break is to work as a QA tester. This entry-level job does not necessarily require a degree, though it is often a designer's first job out of college. It is useful for making contacts in the industry while sharpening valuable skills.

QA testers are usually asked to test a game that is in development. The tester's goal is to try and find all the flaws or bugs so that designers can address them before the game goes to market. "You're trying to break the game," explains Murphy, who worked in QA for many years before becoming a video game designer. "I worked on a golf game, and my job for the first month on the team was to take my player up to every tree on the golf course and try to hit a ball into the tree and make sure . . . that when the ball hit the tree, it would bounce off."[15] If it did not bounce, Murphy had found a bug. He had to take a screen capture of where the tree was and send it to the programming team.

A video game tester's job is to communicate to the development team what the bug is and where it probably came from. Once the bug is fixed, a tester gets the game back to test again and make sure it is gone. "It's almost like detective work," Murphy says. "There's some brainwork involved there."[16]

CHAPTER 3

What Skills and Personal Qualities Matter Most—and Why?

Because video game designers oversee so many different elements of a game—from the concept to the writing and the programming—they need to have a variety of skills. "Designers are often the center point of a big production team," explains Alexandre Charbonneau, lead game designer on *Modern Combat*. "You need to know a little bit of everything. You need to be a good writer, a master communicator, have strong math skills, know how to program and know a bit about art; any extra skills are an advantage in our industry."[17]

Creativity and Technical Knowledge

One of the skills you will need to make it as a video game designer is creativity. Game designers often create entirely new worlds and populate them with invented people or made-up creatures. To come up with story lines and characters and develop them into a game that people will want to play requires a lot of imagination.

"Designers are often the center point of a big production team. You need to know a little bit of everything."[17]

—Alexandre Charbonneau, lead game designer for *Modern Combat*

"You need creativity to have a vision, see what will make a game fun and create a great experience,"[18] says designer Paolo Malabuyo.

Designers must also be innovative enough to come up with ideas that have not been done many times before. For a game to be a hit, the story and characters need to feel fresh and new.

For example, critics panned the 2011 game *Call of Juarez: The Cartel* because the characters and plot felt like they had been done many times before. It did not help that the game was full of glitches, like characters walking through walls.

Designers also need to understand how their concept can be adapted to the available video game platforms and translated into programming code. In addition they need to understand at least the basics of debugging any problems. Doing so requires one to have a background in computer programming or game software development. If a designer is not well versed in technology, he or she might come up with a game concept that is impossible to produce. Although designers do not have to learn programming languages, they need to at least know which languages are available and how they work.

The Well-Rounded Designer

What qualities do video game companies look for in new hires? Veteran video game designer Arnold Hendrick—who has worked on games like *Darklands*, *Pirates! Gold*, and *Marvel Super Hero Squad Online*—says subject- or period-specific knowledge is a must. For example, a designer who wants to work on a historic military game must understand how war was fought and what types of weapons were used in battle during that time period. "A topic-challenged designer may need months to read and research enough to become a semi-expert," Hendrick says. "A designer who is familiar with the subject can immediately start thinking about how subject and game play might converge."

General knowledge is important too. "Designers are more effective if they understand something about graphic design, art, music, and theater," says Hendrick. "The best designers that I know are renaissance men and women with numerous interests and abilities."

Arnold Hendrick, "Hiring Game Designers," Gamasutra, March 20, 1998. www.gamasutra.com.

Game designers have to be able to convey their vision to writers, artists, programmers, and others who will bring the ideas to life. Achieving this requires the ability to make clear presentations to team members.

Communication and Problem-Solving Skills

Once you have a concept for a video game, your job is to convince your company to develop it and then work with a team to get it made. It is thus critical to be able to clearly communicate your ideas, both in speaking and writing. "No idea, no matter how great, will ever come to fruition if you can't get it out of your head and into the heads of the dozens of other people that need to understand it,"[19] says one designer.

Designers must also be able to describe their vision to the writers, artists, programmers, and other people who will work on the game. "A large portion of a game designer's job is design documentation or writing 5,000 e-mails," says Akira Yamaoka, who works for the Japanese entertainment company Konami. "That means you need good technical writing skills and an ability to organize your thoughts. You need to be able to pass a document off to audio, QA, marketing, the programming staff, and an artist, and they should be able to find out whatever information they need just by looking at the document."[20] Clear writing, as well as some proficiency in creating visual aids like diagrams, PowerPoint presentations, and flow charts, can help you express your vision to the team.

Designers must also be skilled problem solvers. Indeed, games are filled with problems, such as quests to achieve and puzzles to crack. As a designer, you will be tasked with creating these problems and making them difficult—but not so difficult that they prevent players from moving forward. Problem solving is an essential skill throughout the game development process because problems inevitably arise at every stage: A story line does not make sense. A bug causes unexpected issues in the game or prevents players from accomplishing a critical task. The game might go over budget or get behind schedule. In every situation, designers need to think quickly and figure out strategies to overcome the issue.

The Role of Math

Though players might not see math in the games they play, it is there. Each time a bird flies through the air, a character jumps up, or a ball rolls down a hill, mathematical formulas determine the trajectory and speed of the movement. In this way, math is foundational to video games.

Each game is based on a series of rules that determine how characters and objects act and move—rules that are based in mathematics. Programmers use formulas to make a character's car drive faster down a track or to come to a halt when it hits a wall. Geometry, for example, is an essential part of every video game. "If you zoomed in on one of the robots, and you zoomed all the way in as far as you could get, underneath everything is a polygon. And that polygon is going to be made up of triangles," says Shaun McCabe, a video game producer for Insomniac Games. "So even at the basest level of something that looks like it's entirely aesthetic, there's still math."[21] Designers must understand the fundamentals of math and how it is used to define the game's parameters.

Animation, Writing, and Sound Design

Animation, writing, and sound design are also all featured in the games designers make. Even if designers do not know how to animate or write a musical score for a game, they should understand how these processes work so they can communicate with the animators, writers, and sound designers who work on the project.

The interactive nature of video games requires more animation, writing, and sound than is required in a television show or movie. In those mediums, all viewers consume the content from the same perspective; that is, everyone watching a movie or a television show experiences the same thing at the same time. However, in a video game, because the player controls the action, user experiences are individualized—and this requires that much more attention be paid to animation, writing, and sound. Characters need to look good from every angle. The story has to be flexible enough to account for the many different decisions a player might make. Extra sound effects must be built in to accommodate these decisions—for example, whether a driver steers a car down a street or off a cliff.

Understanding the Industry—and Your Audience

If a company is going to spend months or years working on a game, not to mention thousands or even millions of dollars, it wants to make sure that game sells. Therefore, successful designers require at least some understanding of the industry—which games are popular right now (or which might become popular in the next few years) and who is playing them. They also need to know which new platforms have become or are about to become available. Is Xbox or PlayStation planning to release a new console with added graphics or functionality that must be built into the game? Designers should be aware of such trends so they can design games that will work on whatever platform is around the corner. Finally, designers must be familiar with their competition—other games on the market that are similar to the one they are developing.

Designers also need to understand what their players want. Designers do not just design the game *they* want to play; they must design the game *everyone else* wants to play. "Designers

Video game designers need to keep up with changes in technology. They should know when updated consoles are coming out and be aware of any advances in graphics or other functions that affect the game-play experience.

with this trait will look for different ways to understand their target audience, to really get inside their heads, and use those insights to craft something great for their players,"[22] says Phil Mansell, studio head and product vice president at Jagex Games Studio.

Personal Qualities

In addition to these skills, designers must have a few personal qualifications too. They must work collaboratively with a team of writers, artists, programmers, and testers. They need the temperament to get along with many personality types and be willing to accept criticism. "Game development is an extremely iterative, collaborative process," says Ken Levine, cofounder of Irrational Games. "A designer who sits off in a corner by himself writing a game design doc is going to be pretty shocked at the reaction he gets when he gives it to the team to 'figure out.'"[23]

Designers must be flexible enough to change course when a game's development is not going as planned. They also need management skills because they are often tasked with overseeing the project from start to finish, often under grueling deadlines and rigid budget constraints. Above all, being a successful video game designer requires dedication and a strong work ethic. "When you're three months from shipping, working until 2 a.m., you need to be pretty darn dedicated,"[24] says Malabuyo.

Creating a video game takes months or years of long hours and hard work. Designers encounter many failures along the way. They might even see a game fail entirely. A positive, can-do attitude helps video game designers get through the inevitable failures, learn from them, and apply them to more successful projects in the future.

CHAPTER 4

What Is It Like to Work as a Video Game Designer?

The video game industry has exploded in recent years, and that means there are ample job opportunities for game designers. A huge variety of positions are available in many different companies. A designer might work at a big game design company, such as Activision Blizzard, Nintendo, or Ubisoft. Or he or she might work for an independent (indie) game developer made up of just a few people. Some designers even start their own business, creating their own games or working independently for other companies as a freelancer or independent contractor. A smaller number of designers work for software companies, media companies, or educational or publishing companies. Some teach game design at colleges and universities.

Working for each type of company has its advantages. Big companies typically offer job security, good benefits, and the chance to work on big-name games like *Paper Mario* or *FIFA Soccer*. However, big firms may not allow you to have much input into a game's design, at least when you are just starting out. You will likely work on a small part of a big game, following the directions of a senior or lead game designer. Designers who work for indie developers typically get a bigger role in the development process. The downside is the volatility. An indie company that is working on only one game can go out of business—and take your job with it—if that game flops.

A Video Game Designer's Typical Day
A typical day for a video game designer is actually anything but typical. "In over 17 years of working in the video game industry I

can't say that I've had a typical working day, which I'm sure is why I still love the job,"[25] says Pete Low, a game designer at Chunk.

What designers do on any given day depends on what projects they are working on and where they are in the project development process. "One day I may be writing up concepts and feature ideas for potential new games, working with other members of the team to focus the vision for a product or communicating with a client to ensure that our goals are clear and headed in the right direction," Low says. "Another day may involve tuning attributes within a game, such as speed, gravity and other forces that dictate how things move and react when a game is interacted with."[26]

Typical tasks involve brainstorming new concepts, developing characters and plots, building three-dimensional models of the game world, or testing and fine-tuning the game. Because game production is a team effort, regular meetings are a big part of the job. Some companies have daily meetings to go over the tasks assigned to each team member and to identify potential problems or bottlenecks in the development process.

Though the work is generally fun and varied, during crunch times when projects are due, the hours can be long and the days grueling. A normal job that typically takes place between the hours of 9 a.m. and 5 p.m. (or even 6 or 7 p.m.) can quickly turn into one that requires someone to put in round-the-clock hours. Even when games are not close to deadline, designers are expected to put in long days, working even after the office has closed. "I stopped tracking my hours because it becomes depressing to think about," says Steve Bowler, lead designer at Phosphor Games. "Most weeks I bet I do 80 hours at a minimum. I'm frequently stealing hours on the weekend to work on my laptop polishing things in the game or writing up a new RFP [request for proposal] or a pitch deck for an upcoming project, and most nights I wind up opening up the editor and working 'til midnight or 1 a.m."[27]

Video game design is not a solitary endeavor. Designers often meet with other team members throughout the design and production process to develop and approve new concepts, characters, and plots.

The Work Atmosphere

In some respects, video game companies are similar to companies in many other industries. Designers work at desks in cubicles and hold team meetings in conference rooms. However, the environment is much more laid-back than is usually found at, say, a law firm or a utility company. Employees can wear jeans or shorts, T-shirts, and flip-flops to work. They are free—and even encouraged—to decorate their cubicles with artwork. And, of course, they can play video games during their workday.

Freelance video game designers have even less structure— they can do their job from their living room in pajamas. Like many other independent contractors, freelancers are not employees of a company, and thus they make their own schedule (though they also are not offered benefits, vacation time, or the other perks typically offered with full-time employment). Although the self-directed aspect of the job can allow a freelancer to skip out for a few hours in the middle of the workweek, some find themselves working through the weekend when a big deadline is looming.

A Day in the Life of a Game Designer

On the *Kingslsle Blog,* Sara Jensen Schubert, lead designer of the game *Pirate101,* shared a typical day at her company, Kingslsle Entertainment:

9:30 a.m.—Schubert arrives at the office and checks e-mail to see if any problems or issues have arisen. She then checks a bug-tracking program to see if any design bugs have come up that the designers need to fix.

10:00 a.m.—Schubert looks in on the designers to see how they are doing.

10:30 a.m.—She goes through more e-mails and keeps an eye out for bugs in the game.

11:30 a.m.—She reviews a new feature with a user interface designer and suggests options to improve it.

12:30 p.m.—Schubert reviews even more e-mails and bug fixes. She plays a game to help another designer fix a boss fight (a fight with the biggest enemy, who usually appears at the end of a game level). She also reads a game design document from another designer and offers feedback.

2:30 p.m.—She discusses a new art idea with the lead artist.

3:00 p.m.—She revises a design document so it can go to art and programming for implementation. She also solves a problem with a feature a programmer is implementing.

4:30 p.m.—Schubert fixes a few bugs.

5:30 p.m.—She plays the game.

6:00 p.m.—She goes home.

Despite the fun environment, game designers must remember they have an important job to do. "Although the atmosphere is casual (t-shirts and jeans, Nerf gun fights, and toys in everyone's cubicle), it is actually very hard and serious work,"[28] says designer David Mullich. Some of it is tedious, as video game designers spend much of their day working in front of a computer. Answering e-mails, writing up design documents, and scripting are big parts of the job. Long hours spent typing on a keyboard—or even playing portions of a game in development—can get repetitive and monotonous.

The video game industry as a whole skews young—and male. By many accounts, the industry is male dominated and not very welcoming toward women. A 2014 survey by the International Game Developers Association found that women occupy just 22 percent of positions in the industry. Female designers earn about 14 percent less than their male counterparts, and some women complain of unequal treatment too. "If you are a woman in the industry, there are all these little signals that you are not part of the club, that this is not your tribe," says Marleigh Norton, cofounder and game developer at Green Door Labs. "After time, it wears you down."[29] With more and more women playing video games (women currently make up 44 percent of gamers in the United States, according to the Entertainment Software Association), the industry's gender divide will hopefully narrow.

> "Although the atmosphere is casual (t-shirts and jeans, Nerf gun fights, and toys in everyone's cubicle), it is actually very hard and serious work."[28]
>
> —Video game designer David Mullich

Earnings

The average video game designer earns more than $73,000 a year, according to Gamasutra's 2014 Game Developer Salary Survey. To start, designers might make closer to $40,000. Once a designer reaches a higher-level position like lead designer or manager, he or she can earn $100,000 or more. Some companies offer profit sharing, an incentive in which employees get a cut of the studio's revenues in addition to their salary. Knowing they might share in the profits motivates some designers to make a game as good as they possibly can. Freelance designers often get paid by the project or the hour. Their ultimate earnings depend on how much each project pays and how many hours they work.

How much one earns as a designer depends on a few factors. One is the number of years a designer has been in the business and what kinds of skills he or she possesses. Programming is a hot commodity, and the high pay reflects the demand. A designer who can also program can earn well over $100,000 annually. The other factor is where in the country a designer lives. Video game companies in big cities like Los Angeles and New York typically pay more than those in smaller cities.

Some big companies offer extra perks, beyond salary and monetary bonuses. For example, the offices of EA Canada—which produces *FIFA Soccer*, *Madden NFL*, and *Bejeweled Stars*—feature a theater, coffee bars, a fitness room, restaurants, and a full-length soccer field for the company's thirteen hundred employees. For some employees, these amenities make coming to work feel a lot less like work.

CHAPTER 5

Advancement and Other Job Opportunities

As in other industries, video game designers typically start in an entry-level position and work their way up. You might begin as a QA tester and then work as a programmer, artist, or writer on another designer's game concept. If you are successful, you can graduate to a job as a video game designer. From there, and once you have experience under your belt, the next step is to become a lead or senior designer. The ultimate goal for many designers is to launch their own video game studio.

There are several positions on the video game design career ladder, and each has its own responsibilities. How quickly someone moves through these levels depends on his or her skills, the job opportunities available, and how hard he or she is willing to work.

Video Game QA Tester

Playing video games on the job sounds like a lot of fun, but testing is actually an integral part of the game development process. Testers get a section of a new game to play over and over again. Their goal is to find any bugs or glitches that might interrupt a player's experience or cause the game to malfunction or misperform. Basically, their job is to try and break the game so designers can fix it.

Being a QA tester involves a lot more than simply playing video games. The work can be tedious and monotonous. Instead of getting to play the entire game as one would at home, testers play just one small part of the game. They test that area over and over for days, weeks, or even months at a time. "Imagine your favorite movie," says Reuben, a video game tester. "Now take your favorite 30-second clip from that movie. Now watch that 30-second clip over and over again, 12 hours a day, every day for two months. When you've done that, tell me if what you've been doing is watching movies all day. I'm willing to bet you'll find that it's not quite the same thing."[30]

However, for someone who truly loves video games and wants a career in the industry, there's no better way to get experience. "If you enjoy tinkering and trying to break things, video game testing could still be potentially a route for you," says Brent Gocke, senior release manager for Sony Computer Entertainment America. "It's for someone who is meticulous, someone who enjoys games and is passionate about playing these things and the different possibilities."[31]

Staff-Level Designer

After gaining QA experience, a person might get hired as a video game designer. Staff-level designers work as a team to create all of a game's elements. This includes the plot, characters, level maps, scenarios, puzzles, and the ways players interact with and win the game. During development, the designer works closely with all the other team members—programmers, writers, and artists—to make sure every piece of the game comes together seamlessly and that there are no bugs.

Designers are often assigned by the senior or lead designer to work on a specific area or part of the game. For example, the lead designer might ask a staff designer to create the layout for a certain level of the game—to put in buildings, trees, and other features. Or he or she might design a move for a certain character. For example, a designer working on a Marvel superheroes game might be tasked with building moves for the Incredible Hulk. This requires the designer to consider how the Hulk hits foes—with his fists? Does he kick them, or charge into them? Depending on the game, such tasks can be incredibly creative or feel small and repetitive. "You're doing a lot of the low-level work that may be interesting, or it may be super dull. It just depends on the job,"[32] says video game designer Kelly Murphy.

Once a designer has developed a character's move set or

Tips for Landing a Job in Game Design

The competitive nature of the video game industry can make landing your first job a challenge. Here are a few strategies to help you navigate the interview process and improve your odds of getting hired:

Know the company. Do your research. Visit the company's website or a gaming news site. Learn the history of the company, which games they have released, and who the senior members of the team are. Also do a little digging about the people who are going to interview you. Find out where they went to school and what games they have personally worked on.

Know the game. If you are interviewing to work on a specific game, learn everything you can about it. If it is part of a franchise like FIFA or Mario, play previous games in the series. Make a note of what you liked or thought needed improvement (but avoid being overly critical).

Bring demos. Develop a portfolio of games you have worked on and be prepared to show it. Be honest about your role in each project, however. Do not say you were the game's lead designer if you did QA.

Follow up. After your interview, send a thank-you e-mail to each person you spoke with. Let them know how nice it was to meet them, how excited you are at the prospect of working for their company, and what you think you can contribute.

other game feature, he or she must explain how the feature works to the rest of the team. Then, after the programmers and other team members have implemented the feature, the designer plays it, testing it to make sure it works and trying out possible solutions where it does not. This is one of the many ways in which the video game designer job involves a lot of trial and error. "We iterate [go over and over] on something 100 times before it's right. Even if we've done it before," says designer Steve Bowler. "I worked on making an AI [artificial intelligence] animate properly as it dropped off a ledge. It took me five hours and I had to reach out to two people for help thinking through the problem."[33]

Senior/Lead Designer

Once designers have experience as a video game designer, they can move up to senior or lead designer. At this level, they work on the objectives for one or more levels of the game they are developing. Then they will create a document outlining those objectives for other team members to follow.

The job of a senior or lead designer is not much different from that of a regular designer, with the exception that he or she oversees a bigger part of the project. The lead designer creates a plan that includes decisions about how the game will look and work—including the scenes, characters, story, rules, and interface. He or she also writes the documentation that keeps the team pointed in the same direction as they work on their various tasks, and interfaces with artists and programmers to map out each element of the game.

Throughout the process, the lead designer is responsible for making sure team members are achieving their assigned tasks and that the game development stays on schedule and budget. He or she also addresses any issues that arise while developing or testing the game.

Senior Manager of Game Design

The senior manager is in charge of making the high-level decisions as a video game is being developed. He or she decides what the game will be about and how it will look and play. Once the game is in development, the senior manager supervises each team member to make sure that the piece he or she is working on sticks to the company's goals for the game.

Rising to the senior manager level means taking on more responsibility and having more control over the game's vision. However, it also means doing less hands-on work in terms of designing the elements of the game. "If you value working on the game and making the game, as you move up it's kind of a struggle because you're less hands on," says Murphy of senior positions. "It's more decision making."[34]

Moving Through the Ranks

The demand for video games is increasing exponentially. Game sales rose to $23.5 billion in 2015, a 5 percent leap from the previous year, according to the Entertainment Software Association. That means advancement opportunities for talented game designers are plentiful. However, thanks to the huge popularity of video games, this industry is also highly competitive. It can be hard to even land a first job, let alone get promoted. You might have to make a few detours along the way. "Don't be discouraged if you don't get a job in games straight away," says developer Kerry Turner. "I started out making educational software by day and working on short experimental games in the evenings. These personal projects became my portfolio, which eventually landed me a job making games."[35]

Any advantage you can give yourself will increase your odds of landing a first job and moving up the ranks. To improve your prospects, learn as many skills as you can. Get proficient in a few programming and scripting languages. Even if you are working in an entry-level QA position, build your own games on the side. You can feature these games in your portfolio when you interview for higher-level positions. You can also enhance your profile and visibility online. Start your own website to showcase your games. Write a blog or articles about the gaming industry and your own work within it, and submit it to sites like *That Videogame Blog* or *Engadget*.

> "I started out making educational software by day and working on short experimental games in the evenings. These personal projects became my portfolio, which eventually landed me a job making games."[35]
>
> —Developer Kerry Turner

The ultimate goal for many video game designers is to start their own studio. The best way to do that is to learn all you can about the industry by spending at least a few years working for an established company. "Meet people, learn how you work and how games work, learn the dynamics," suggests Rhodri Broadbent, cofounder of Dakko Dakko Ltd. "Then set up [your own studio] when you get a good feel for what sort of studio you want to make."[36]

CHAPTER 6

What Does the Future Hold for Video Game Designers?

Video game industry insiders have good news about the future of gaming. According to the advisory and consulting firm PwC, the industry is projected to grow 30 percent by 2019. Video games are expected to increase in popularity faster than any other form of entertainment, including television, music, and books.

The success of the video game market is due in part to the increasing number of platforms on which to play them. Today you can play video games on your television, computer, console, handheld device, smartphone, or tablet. You can even play them 35,000 feet (10,668 m) in the sky on an airplane. The more platforms there are for games, the more people will play them. "It seems pretty clear . . . that gaming begets gaming: console gamers are more likely to pick up mobile games, and vice versa,"[37] says video game and technology writer Dave Thier. Gaming has expanded outside the typical uses too. Schools, the military, and corporations now use video games as a training tool, further expanding the market for designers.

Players may not realize it, but they help determine which genres and games will be the next big thing by making choices about which games to buy and play. "The future of gaming will not be all that different than the future of any other form of entertainment," says video game journalist Michael

> "The future of gaming will not be all that different than the future of any other form of entertainment. As the masses of players determine what they want to get out of gaming, large corporations will throw their money and workforce into providing it."[38]
>
> —Video game journalist Michael Dolan

The gaming industry is growing rapidly, which is good news for people interested in game design or other jobs in the industry. New platforms allow people to play almost anywhere, including on airplanes.

Dolan. "As the masses of players determine what they want to get out of gaming, large corporations will throw their money and workforce into providing it."[38] That increased workforce will likely create many new opportunities for video game designers.

New Technologies

Video games have come a long way since the early 1970s, when a ball bounced between two white lines against a black background in *Pong*. Many of today's video games are three-dimensional and highly realistic. Some even allow the user to step inside the game. The introduction of virtual reality (VR) and augmented reality (AR) technologies has been among the most exciting and most promising recent developments in gaming. In VR, the player is fully immersed in the video game experience. With VR technologies like the Oculus Rift headset, players interact within a fully three-dimensional world—as if they were inside the game. "Once the goggles were in place . . . I was instantly inside the cockpit of a military space fighter, launching into a gloomy, asteroid-filled galaxy of hostile aliens and impossibly vast ships," describes Business Insider editor Jim Edwards of his experience playing a VR game. "It is one of those rare products where describing it in mere words doesn't come anywhere near to realistically depicting how incredible the experience of wearing one is."[39]

In AR, the game adds graphics, sounds, and other computer-generated elements to the real world. An example of AR is the *Pokémon Go* mobile game, which debuted in July 2016. At the peak of its popularity, *Pokémon Go* had millions of people around the globe searching parks, stores, restaurants, and even their own homes to find and catch more than one hundred different species of these virtual creatures.

The success of *Pokémon Go* is inspiring the next generation of AR games. "Our team predicts that other franchises will emerge once again with the rise of these new generation AR games," Asem Syed writes on the Technobyte website. "Mario searching different castles for the Princess. Popeye finding spinach boxes to knock out Bluto. Or even Tom scouting different locations for Jerry and his cousins. The possibilities are endless."[40]

Gaming Events

With the growth of online gaming comes the opportunity to attract bigger and bigger audiences for games. The global nature of the Internet will enable millions of people around the world to play or watch games at the same time. Game companies will "try to create massive shared experiences online," says Dolan. "They'll launch 'must see' events in an attempt to draw millions of players online simultaneously."[41]

One example of such an event is an eSport competition—the video game equivalent of World Cup soccer or NBA basketball. In an eSport event, a crowd gathers in an arena and viewers from around the world watch from their home computers as teams or individual video game players take part in high-stakes gaming competitions. Andrew Paradise, chief executive officer of the mobile eSports start-up Skillz, predicts that eSport events will soon rival leagues like the NFL and NBA in popularity and viewership. "Imagining a day when eSports competitions share the same stage as premier sporting events like the Super Bowl and March Madness is not far-fetched," he says. "The data backs it up."[42]

The Rise of Indie Game Studios

The gaming industry today is going through a shift similar to what the film industry went through a couple of decades ago. In the film industry, big studios used to reign supreme. Then independent studios started taking over. Their ability to work with smaller budgets allowed them to push the boundaries of creative filmmaking. Over time, independent films became increasingly popular.

A similar movement has taken place in the gaming industry. In the 1990s, indie games started out as a kind of hobby for certain designers. Independent developers tried to make the kinds of games they wanted to play, rather than games that would simply earn lots of money, as the big companies were doing. At first, indie game creation was more of a cottage industry. Individuals or little groups of developers sold only small numbers of games because they could not afford the marketing and distribution needed to get them out to huge audiences. A big turning point occurred around 2008, when developers no longer had to spend huge amounts of money to produce and package an actual game disc to be sold in physical stores. For the first time, Internet-based platforms like Steam allowed them to distribute their games online, inexpensively. These new distribution channels gave indie developers the chance to get their games out to a huge audience at very low cost.

Some of the most successful indie games are today household names. In 2011 Swedish programmer Markus "Notch" Persson and his company, Mojang, released the independent game

"Imagining a day when eSports competitions share the same stage as premier sporting events like the Super Bowl and March Madness is not far-fetched. The data backs it up."[42]

—Andrew Paradise, CEO of mobile eSports start-up Skillz

Team members take part in a competitive gaming tournament. Many of these competitions attract a global audience of millions; spectators usually watch the action from their home computers.

Minecraft. The point of the game was to collaboratively build castles, skyscrapers, and other structures using textured blocks. *Minecraft* went on to sell more than 100 million copies, making it the most successful indie game to date. In 2009, indie studio Rovio introduced the mobile game *Angry Birds*. Within a year consumers had downloaded 12 million copies from the Apple app store. *Minecraft*, *Angry Birds*, and games like them have opened the door for independent game developers like Frogdice, Frictional Games, and 2D Boy.

The move toward indie studios has given young video game designers the chance to express their creativity and have a bigger

Video Game Stars

Video game designers do not sit around and play video games all day, but some members of a growing new side profession do. They are gamers who have turned their passion into a high-paying job and have become huge stars in the process.

Smosh (a duo composed of Anthony Padilla and Ian Hecox), PewDiePie, Markiplier, and GameGrumps are just a few of the celebrities who are responsible for creating a whole new entertainment medium. They play video games on YouTube while making funny comments and adding music and animation to the mix. These Internet stars have racked up millions of followers and dollars. PewDiePie, whose real name is Felix Kjellberg, currently has nearly 49 million YouTube subscribers and earns approximately $2.2 million a year. Some of these gamers are so famous that they even influence game sales. In fact, PewDiePie's popularity "has been likened to the Oprah's book club, where anything he touches gets a boost in sales," writes ZOG Digital marketing coordinator Michael Pasco.

Michael Pasco, "YouTube Star's Influence Beyond the Video Platform," *Huffington Post*, September 9, 2015. www.huffingtonpost.com.

say in the game development process. "The great news is anyone with a passion for creativity can have a go at creating video games," writes digital marketing expert Alex Morris. "Funding can come from services such as Kickstarter, but thousands of passionate indie developers often work on projects in their spare time and release titles for free. Success can lead to titles finding their way to digital distribution platforms like Steam or they can be picked up for console or mobile publication."[43]

A Bright Future in Gaming

The evolution to virtual and three-dimensional entertainment has increased the need for highly creative and technologically adept video game designers. As technologies like VR, AR, and mobile games further develop and new technologies emerge, the future for video game designers will be virtually limitless. Independent publishing platforms like Steam are giving anyone with the desire to create his or her own games the opportunity to do so. As a result of these developments, talented, hardworking designers will be able to go as far in this industry as their imaginations—and dreams—will allow them.

Interview with a Video Game Designer

Kelly Murphy is a video game designer who spent ten years at Disney and now works for an augmented reality gaming company called castAR. He spoke with the author about his career.

Q: How did you get into video game design?

A: I went to Ball State University in Indiana, where I was an art major. Then I transferred to the University of Utah to finish school, and I got a degree in film. My final year in college I was waiting tables, and I hated it. There was a game studio about a block away from the restaurant. I walked down there on my break one day and asked them if they had any quality assurance positions open. They had me fill out an application and then they called me a couple weeks later for an interview and offered me the job. That was my break into the industry.

I did QA while I finished school, and then afterward I worked for Acclaim, which was a big video game publisher in the 1990s and early 2000s. After a year of that, I did QA for Microsoft for about four years. Then I got a design job with them. That was my introduction into video game design.

Then I went to Disney, and I was a staff-level designer. I got promoted to senior designer a few years in, and then lead designer. Senior manager of game design was my last title at Disney. I stopped working there in May when they shut the studio down. Now I work for a company called castAR. They do augmented reality gaming.

Q: Can you describe your typical workday?

A: My day depends on where I am in a project. In an early pre-production phase, I spend any time I have researching. Let's say I was working on Spiderman's combat move set. I would do research by playing some best-in-class games that were similar to the type of game we were trying to make. I'd take notes about what I liked, what I didn't like, and why. Then I would brainstorm. I would say, "Ok, I've got Spiderman. That's my central character." Then I would branch off and say, "He's agile, he's really strong, and he's got webs."

From there, I would start thinking about Spiderman's moves and documenting them visually. I might have a document with a picture of the controller on it. And then I'd type near the controller buttons the names of moves—like a punch, kick, or dodge. My end goal would be to come up with a proposed move set design with some detail about how the moves work and how they're limited. I would take that document to my lead designer, go over it with him or her, get feedback, and then revise. The ultimate goal would be to take the moves to the team and pitch them to the artists, animators, and programmers—the people who were going to make the game—get their feedback and revise it. And then finally we'd get them into production.

Q: What do you like most about your job?

A: One of the things I love is the people. I really love getting to know the team I work with, figuring out what motivates everyone on my team, and then trying to foster a really good relationship with each of them.

Being creative within a box is also a fun thing for me. If you were to tell me just to make a game, I would have a harder time than if you said, "We have this box. Make a game within this box." I worked for Disney for ten years. All the games I did except for one were based on preexisting licenses like Marvel and Star Wars. It's fun to try to be clever within a box. The problem-solving aspects of that are really cool.

Q: What do you like least about your job?

A: Timelines. You never have the time you want as a creative. You're always fighting for resources, whether it's time or people. The business side will push you to get the game done as quickly as you can.

Also, the hours are insane. That's something people need to be prepared for if they're looking to get into the industry. I probably spent a majority of my thirties at work. When you're young, that's cool. It doesn't really matter. As you get older and you have a family, it gets very hard.

Q: What personal qualities do you think are most valuable for someone to have in this profession?

A: You have to be a critical thinker, self-motivated, and curious. Also have interests other than games. The best designers in the world have hobbies like gardening, travel, or music. And that's really good. That's healthy. Having exposure to the outside world helps you come up with new ideas for your games.

Q: What advice do you have for students who might be interested in becoming a game designer?

A: The first thing to start doing is to go home and play the games you love. Ask yourself what you like and don't like about them, and why. And ask what you haven't seen in a game that you'd want to play. Start practicing critical thinking with your entertainment.

Then start creating within the games you have. Now kids have access to tools that are really powerful. A lot of games, like *Minecraft*, allow you to build whole games. Come up with an idea and try to build it. You'll learn which tools you wish you had. And you're going to get better with the tools you do have. That's going to help you cross the gap between consumer and creator.

Once you've done that, download the Unity game development platform and start doing tutorials. Create your own games and share them. Post them to Facebook, Twitter, and other social media sites to get them out there.

SOURCE NOTES

Introduction: Life as a Video Game Designer

1. Quoted in Ryan Daws, "#MWC16: How the Game Industry Is Evolving," Developer Tech, February 26, 2016. www.developer-tech.com.
2. Quoted in AllArtSchools, "Video Game Designer Profile: Paolo Malabuyo." www.allartschools.com.
3. Quoted in RPGamer, "Breaking Into the Industry: An Interview with Tomm Hulett." www.rpgamer.com.

Chapter 1: What Does a Video Game Designer Do?

4. Quoted in Eric Lipsky, "Game Designer Interview: What Do Game Designers Do?," Schools.com, April 14, 2015. www.schools.com.
5. Quoted in Stephen Totilo, "Creating a Video Game with Nintendo Sounds Stressful, Amazing, and Unreal," *Kotaku* (blog). http://kotaku.com.
6. Quoted in Lipsky, "Game Designer Interview."
7. Matt Spiel, "Interview: Game Designer—Jake Fleming," *Team Treehouse* (blog), July 7, 2014. http://blog.teamtreehouse.com.

Chapter 2: How Do You Become a Video Game Designer?

8. Kelly Murphy, interview with author, September 25, 2016.
9. Murphy, interview.
10. Murphy, interview.
11. Quoted in Tristan Donovan, "To Play or Not to Play?," Gamasutra, September 27, 2011. www.gamasutra.com.
12. Allen Varney, "Game Design FAQ." www.allenvarney.com.
13. Quoted in Dennis Nishi, "Intern to Civilization Leader," *Wall Street Journal*, June 29, 2010. www.wsj.com.
14. Quoted in Kat Shanahan, "Get to Know a Game Designer: An Interview with Abby Friesen," *Inside Filament* (blog), Filament Games, September 28, 2015. www.filamentlearning.com.

15. Murphy, interview.
16. Murphy, interview.

Chapter 3: What Skills and Personal Qualities Matter Most—and Why?

17. Quoted in *Modern Combat 4*, "Interview: Lead Game Designer," November 23, 2012. www.modern-combat.net.
18. Quoted in AllArtSchools, "Video Game Designer Profile."
19. Quoted in JobMonkey, "Interview: Skills Video Game Designers Need." www.jobmonkey.com.
20. Quoted in Bob Colayco, "So You Wanna Be a Game Designer," GameSpot, July 22, 2005. www.gamespot.com.
21. Quoted in Scaling Up STEM Learning with the VCL, "Video Game Production and Design—Shaun McCabe," YouTube, October 26, 2011. www.youtube.com.
22. Quoted in Craig Chapple, "The Top Five Traits of Must-Have Game Designers," *Develop*, January 2, 2014. www.develop-online.net.
23. Quoted in Colayco, "So You Wanna Be a Game Designer."
24. Quoted in AllArtSchools, "Video Game Designer Profile."

Chapter 4: What Is It Like to Work as a Video Game Designer?

25. Quoted in Chris Lake, "A Day in the Life of a . . . Games Designer," *EConsultancy Blog*, June 18, 2013. https://econsultancy.com.
26. Quoted in Lake, "A Day in the Life of a . . . Games Designer."
27. Quoted in Andy Orin, "Career Spotlight: What I Do as a Game Designer," *Lifehacker* (blog), May 6, 2015. http://lifehacker.com.
28. David Mullich, "What Is Daily Life/a Typical Day Like, Working at a Video Game Company?," Quora, October 12, 2014. www.quora.com.
29. Quoted in Leah Burrows, "Women Remain Outsiders in the Video Game Industry," *Boston Globe*, January 27, 2013. www.bostonglobe.com.

Chapter 5: Advancement and Other Job Opportunities

30. Quoted in Jimmy Thang, "The Tough Life of a Games Tester," IGN, March 29, 2012. www.ign.com.
31. Michelle Castillo, "So You Want to Be a Video Game Tester?," *Time*, December 29, 2010. http://techland.time.com.
32. Murphy, interview.
33. Quoted in Orin, "Career Spotlight."
34. Murphy, interview.
35. Quoted in Keith Stuart, "How to Get into the Games Industry— an Insiders' Guide," *Guardian*, March 20, 2014. www.the guardian.com.
36. Quoted in Stuart, "How to Get into the Games Industry."

Chapter 6: What Does the Future Hold for Video Game Designers?

37. Dave Thier, "Mobile Isn't the Future of Gaming (and Consoles Aren't Either)," *Forbes*, May 15, 2015. www.forbes.com.
38. Michael Dolan, "The Future of Video Gaming," *The Video Game Revolution,* PBS. www.pbs.org.
39. Jim Edwards, "Mere Words Can't Do Justice to How Awesome It Is Inside the Oculus Rift Gaming Headset Facebook Just Bought," Business Insider, March 25, 2014. www.busi nessinsider.com.
40. Asem Syed, "Pokemon Go and a New Generation of Games to Come," Technobyte, August 7, 2016. www.technobyte .org.
41. Dolan, "The Future of Video Gaming."
42. Andrew Paradise, "eSports: On Par with the NFL and NBA?," Recode, December 2, 2015. www.recode.net.
43. Alex Morris, "How the Rise of Indie Games Has Revitalized the Video Game Industry," AllBusiness.com. www.allbusiness .com.

FIND OUT MORE

Entertainment Software Association (ESA)

601 Massachusetts Ave. NW, Suite 300
Washington, DC 20001
www.theesa.com

The ESA is an association for companies that make video games. It runs trade shows and does research on the state of the gaming industry. The ESA website also contains a list of schools that offer video game degree programs, with links to their websites.

Game Center

http://gamecenter.nyu.edu

The website of New York University's Game Center, part of its Department of Game Design, has information about academic coursework and exhibitions, game design workshops, competitions, and conferences. It also provides information on the university's Game Center Incubator, which helps students develop their games for the marketplace.

GameSpot

www.gamespot.com

This comprehensive gaming website offers news, product reviews, and discussion boards for gamers. Keeping up with this site can help you spot the latest trends in the industry. You can also get tips from working video game designers on the forum pages.

IGN

www.ign.com

IGN is a media company that focuses on the video game industry. It offers news, reviews, and blogs that cover many different types of game formats. You can also subscribe to its newsletter to get the latest game news delivered to your inbox.

International Game Developers Association (IGDA)

19 Mantua Rd.
Mt. Royal, NJ 08061
www.igda.org

The IGDA is an organization for people who create video games. It helps video game designers and other professionals connect with their peers and develop their craft.

Values at Play

www.valuesatplay.org

This website is aimed at helping designers to be more intentional about integrating diversity and human values into games and game-based systems. Students can explore game tools, curriculum, research and resources, and plenty of video interviews with experts in the field.

INDEX

PICTURE CREDITS

ABOUT THE AUTHOR

Stephanie Watson is a freelance writer based in Providence, Rhode Island. For nearly two decades she has covered the latest health and science research for online and print publications such as WebMD, Healthline, and *Harvard Women's Health Watch*. Watson has also authored more than two dozen books for young adults, including *The Future of Technology: What Is the Future of Self-Driving Cars?* and *Forgotten Youth: Incarcerated Youth*.